"**How to do Housing**" first UK edition 2021

First published in Great Britain in 2021 by Redpump Ltd. Copyright © Chris Worth 2021.

The right of Chris Worth to be identified as the author of this work is asserted with all rights reserved.

This print perfect bound print edition 1 of How to do Housing is ISBN 978-1-912795-33-8

See <u>100days100grand.com</u>

"You will live to see man-made horrors beyond your comprehension."

—Nikola Tesla

(Obviously saw where the housing market was going)

WHAT IS HOUSING?	9
WHAT HOUSING IS NOT	12
THE HOUSING NON-MARKET	13
THE TYRANNY OF PLANNING	17
The macro level: planning pandemonium	18
The meso level: zoning zombies	19
The micro level: dictating decor	20
A parable: the cage men of Hong Kong	21
INTRODUCING NEVILLE	23
1. Bribery and construction	25
2. Negotiation by navigation	27
3. Sidestep the structures	30
SINGAPORE: CLEAN LIVING	32
Right-to-buy: a great opportunity missed	35
JOY IN THE SLUMS	37
A SOLUTION FOR HOUSING	40
HOUSING AS A SERVICE	42
FROM CODE TO GUIDE	48
1. Remove planning restrictions	51
2. Remove government bungs	54
3. Remove taxes	56
3a. … including taxes on landlords	57

4. Lose adverse aversions	60
5. Think Tiny	62
(... and the stopgap solution)	64
(and make better use of architects)	66
ADDENDUM	67
Going Tiny	68
Containing yourself	70
Vanlife	72
TICKET TO TOKYO	74
ABOUT CHRIS	78

As an itinerant copywriter, I've lived in plenty of places. A 110sqft room in Hong Kong. A Tokyo house made of paper. Large townhouses in London, a hotel in Las Vegas, and many more.

Very different places. But all "home". And always the first To-Do when I move to a new city. Having somewhere to sleep, stay safe, store your stuff is fundamental to moving forward in life.

But there's a problem with housing today. In the places people want to live, ==housing just costs too much==.

In many cities, rentals cost half the average after-tax income. When buying, transaction costs like the UK's Stamp Duty and the USA's property taxes inflate first-year costs by 15% or more. And for those brave souls who want to *build*, a thicket of regulations means a small family home can take twice as long to obtain official approvals as it does to construct.

There's a reason for this. Like most sectors awash in rules and regs, the housing market is distorted—making it easier to game the system. And once something becomes gameable, it's of more use as a speculative investment than for its original purpose. Indeed, the whole housing crisis could be summarised as the difference between a free market price and a distorted, gamed one.

Now there's nothing wrong with treating property as an investment if you have spare cash. (One reason my "big book" on freelancing 100 Days, 100 Grand focusses on boosting your income*. Money solves most things.) But when prices are the result of artificial factors like over-regulation, instead of genuine supply and demand, it's a problem.

Yet it's astonishing how easy such problems can be to solve with some straightforward ideas and plain talk. (At least in principle.) This little book—the latest in a series proposing simple solutions to complex problems like healthcare, welfare, and education—attempts to do so.

Whether or you agree with my solution, I hope these few pages open your eyes to what's *really* making it so difficult for you to find a decent place to live.

CHRIS WORTH

* 100days100grand.com.

WHAT IS HOUSING?

Blues singers excepted, home isn't wherever you lay your hat. Or a cabin in the woods. Or even a suburban McMansion.

Housing is a *psychological imperative*. (In a sense, it *is* where the heart is.)

It's among the first steps on Maslow's Hierarchy of Needs: one of the basic things you need to take care of before you can concentrate on anything else. It's why—for most people—housing is such a huge decision, and so difficult to get right.

And why it's always on the political agenda, even in a world that enables longer commutes, fewer geographical constraints, and more choices than ever.

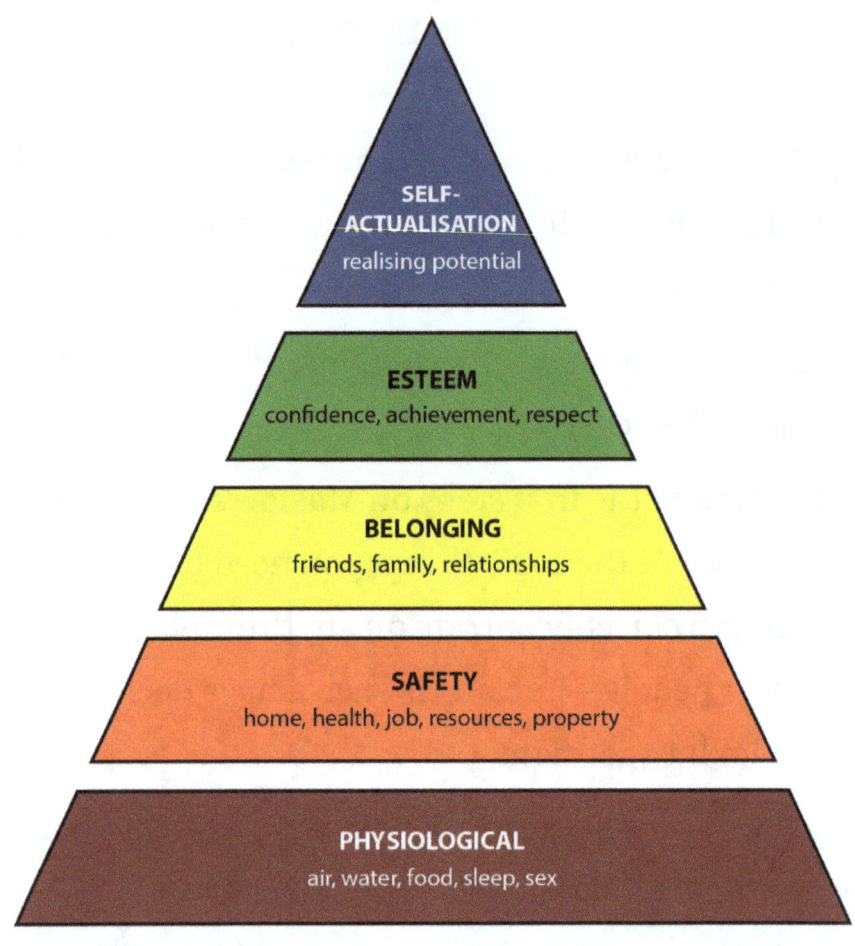

Figure 1: Maslow's Hierarchy of Needs

The great problem with housing is that governments love to define what a "home" is, and guard their definition jealously. And the outcome is rarely one that appeals to the heart.

It's why across Russia, generations have lived in soulless concrete blocks, always five storeys tall so none would need an elevator. Why the USA's housing projects invariably fall victim to drugs and crime. Why the problems of Paris's banlieues seem so intractable.

Yes, they're "housing". But rarely "homes". A home is more than a roof over your head; it's a stake in your own future, an enablement that lets you plan your life.

So housing is your lever, a place to stand from which you can move the Earth. Next, let's define what it *isn't*.

WHAT HOUSING IS NOT

Whatever many politicians might like to think, housing is not a "right". Because nothing can be a right if exercising that right means other people have to provide you with stuff.

(Rights can be positive, like a "right" to food or income—which somebody else must provide—or negative, like the right to be not be murdered. Only negative rights—those not requiring anyone else to take action—are genuine rights.)

Housing is vital to most people's idea of a worthwhile life. But fundamental to solving the housing crisis is that it's a nice-to-have—not a right.

THE HOUSING NON-MARKET

"Everything is scarce" is a basic principle of economics. In fact, *the* basic principle. It's scarcity that lets the price mechanism match demand with supply; it's scarcity that pushes entrepreneurs to compete and innovate; it's scarcity that makes better use of resources when creating value. Scarcity, in economic terms, is a *good* thing.

However, governments don't like scarcity. Because governments get elected by promising *abundance*, paid for by whatever variant of the Magical Money Tree is in vogue: endless free goods and services, fluttering down in unlimited quantity from on high.

You can't blame them: it's a popular message on the

stump. So politicians don't understand scarcity is a Good Thing, and proclaim housing should be provided for all at government largesse. Which means all over the world, governments play a big role in the housing market.

And—of course—royally screw it up.

==In fact, this is the Gordian knot of the housing problem: people think *more* government intervention is needed, when in fact government involvement is what's causing it all.==

Think about it from the perspective of anyone trying to construct a building on land they own. Government defines what you may build. Where you may build it. What materials you can use. How tall it can be. How buyers may use it. What giveaways, sorry, "affordable units", you have to throw in to get permission to start. And—increasingly—what kind of people can live in it and what kind of approved lifestyles they may lead. ("Key worker": the most classist language ever defined. *All* workers are key.)

Compliance with all these regulations carries costs. Both actual, and opportunity. Because each new regulation, every permission slip, limits the value the developer can provide to you, the customer.

And when you *do* find a house you can afford, you have to pay a further extortion fee to government for the privilege of moving in, like the UK's Stamp Duty. Or pay one every month, like the USA's property taxes.

This is not a "market". It's more like a *racket*. Yet it's been happening for so long, with progress towards complete government control so inexorable, that most people believe the housing shortage is a fault with *capitalism.*

Let's be clear: the reason you can't afford the house you want is because of too much government control.

Let's see if there's anything we can do about that.

THE TYRANNY OF PLANNING

There's a standard white elephant argument when it comes to government control over planning: "Without all our regulations, wouldn't there be uncontrolled sprawl, slums, risks?"

That'd be a valid argument, *if* centuries of doing it had solved the housing problem once and for all. But a stroll around any town centre will reveal a thousand failures at all three levels.

==Government is not an all-seeing eye==. Yet as in so many other areas, it considers itself infallible.

It's a premise that starts with absolute control—and creates absolute chaos. On three levels. Let's call them micro-, meso-, and macro-.

The macro level: planning pandemonium

The **macro level** is *central* planning: not the minutiae of bricks and mortar, but the large-scale layouts of cities and neighbourhoods.

When done with purpose and talent, it has its merits, as all Big Picture thinking can. The clear layouts of DC and NYC are a delight; the boulevards of Baron Haussmann make Paris breathtaking. But for every Manhattan there's a Canberra or a Brasilia: the bleached bones of a city ignorant of its inhabitants.

People may cry there's a need for such thinking at scale. But this assumes government does it better than the market—which is a false premise.

The meso level: zoning zombies

At the **meso** is the question of what you do with blocks and neighbourhoods, coming down to **zoning**. It's probably the most pernicious of the three levels. Because while central planning at least looks forward, and building regulations attempt to keep people safe, zoning concepts are utterly artificial: separating where people work from where they live satisfies no market need. And makes for boring cities to boot.

Zoning is what lets old industrial districts decay because their use can't be changed, fills High Streets with charity shops, and forces people to live in cookie-cutter 'burbs far from the fun. Zoning sucks.

The micro level: dictating decor

Zooming into the zones, the **micro** level concerns the buildings themselves: what you're allowed to build and what you can build it with. This crushes another pillar of free markets: their ability to **innovate**.

Britain's "Building Regulations" take up three metres of shelf space; there's a manual just for using it. In the USA, construction is (like many job titles) licensed by State, reducing supply and encouraging cartels. New materials and methods take years to get approved; established ones enjoy quasi-monopolies of supply. While a forest of certificates, permits, and approvals slows down and adds costs to every project. All market-killers. Next: a side story.

A parable: the cage men of Hong Kong

In 1990s Hong Kong, a story popped up on the pages of the South China Morning Post. The "cage men" were poor citizens whose only home was a bunk enclosed by chickenwire, stacked three high in small two- or three-bedroom apartments turned into rabbit warrens for human beings.

This, of course, was illegal. But the story's thrust wasn't about law: it was about the indignity of mostly older Chinese with little education or family living that way.

So questions were raised, the authorities moved in, and soon the men were out of their cages.

Problem solved? Not quite.

Hundreds of people who at least had a roof over their head were now out on the street. At the bottom of the housing market already, they'd had no other choice. The chickenwire hadn't been a cage to them: it was a way to keep their few possessions safe while they were at work.

Cages weren't a great housing option. But they *were* an option, and the free market had provided them. (It's what markets do.) It turned out many of the cage dwellers could have afforded better housing, yet preferred to have more disposable income to send back to their families. However well meant, government do-gooding took away that choice.

And it's all the fault of Neville.

INTRODUCING NEVILLE

The man doing all this damage isn't a natural born killer. Despite his evil deeds, he's probably kind to his family, cooks on Sundays, likes walking the dog.

But he's among the most evil men who ever lived. Because he's the public official you have to kowtow to every time you want to create a building.

Let's call him "Neville".

There are millions of Nevilles around the world. However friendly he looks, his salary, his pension, and Fido's dinner treats depend on him keeping his system of permits and approvals going, creating more work for government departments and therefore a justification for those departments to get bigger and more powerful.

". . . these people are still a part of that system, and that makes them our enemy."—Morpheus, "The Matrix"

Neville's not there to help you, or provide a "service" that "enables" your build. He's there to make things worse.

That's the first clue to our solution: we've got to put paid to the Nevilles. Three methods suggest themselves. Bribe him, game the system, or—best case—do an end-run around him, by making him irrelevant. But would any of them work? Let's look at each option in turn.

1. Bribery and construction

The simplest way to get results out of a public official is to simply pay him off. It's the way of the world, and has been for millennia. Vast sectors of every capital city, from London's Canary Wharf to Mumbai's business districts, owe their existence to the avarice of petty officials.

Of course, many countries have passed laws against this. But there are more creative ways to gain a civil servant's assent than passing over a brown envelope.

You can promise to build things of "benefit to society", like extra units in a housing block. You can offer to pay for public infrastructure, like maintaining a road. Or you can let slip that a new street or building *might* be named after him.

All these methods work. Trouble is, they still leave you squarely within the system: prone to its regulations and in thrall to its insiders. You're still a knave, tugging your forelock before someone with a title. And of course, when you compromise a public official you've also compromised *yourself*. (He'll have as much dirt on you as you have on him.)

So bribery—or whatever synonym you use for it, like "socially beneficial accompaniments"—may solve the odd thing on a project-by-project basis. But it isn't a solution to doing housing *right*.

2. Negotiation by navigation

The second way to deal with any public official is to game the system to your advantage, finding loopholes within the rules without asking Neville to do you any favours.

In some 12th-century European cities, taxes were levied on square footage at ground level. So builders made the upper floors bigger than the ground, leading to buildings on opposite sides of the street that almost touched at higher levels. Developers got their square footage, and Europe got some interesting architecture.

In New York today "pencil towers" proliferate: absurdly narrow skyscrapers. They exist because development rights allow lower-rise buildings to sell "air rights" (permission to grow taller) to neighbouring lots. Once a developer has accumulated enough air rights, he can build a very high tower on a very small lot. (The views must be awesome.)

That's gaming. Seeing regulation in terms of its loopholes, hewing to the letter of the law rather than its spirit. (And hiring some clever lawyers.)

Every rules-based system of any size contains opportunities for gaming. By definition, no centrally-planned solution can catch every one, because the central planning itself *creates* the loopholes. The bigger and more over-reaching the system gets, the more holes and tears there are to scurry through.

Now, developers are rarely angels. But it's clear where the Original Sin is here: the rules that permit such gaming in the first place. As such, gaming the system can't be a sustainable solution either.

3. Sidestep the structures

Even in the developed USA, there are millions of acres of land outside the authority of, well, authorities. Places where you can build without restriction. (And, according to some novels, where crimes can be committed without consequence.)

Across Europe it's rarer, but it still exists, particularly in the extreme South and North. And in Africa and Asia it's commonplace.

So this is the most adventurous of our three ideas: step outside the boundaries of the system, and build the home (or castle) you want.

But this too, has issues. Such areas may lack stultifying laws—but also lack laws that protect you.

And they tend to be far from desirable neighbourhoods: deserts, jungles, the frozen north.

So while there's a certain caché to living the frontiersman lifestyle, it's also cutting you off from economic opportunities. You'll be free of the Nevilles. But you'll also be free of the better things in life, like home-delivered pizza.

So what *can* be done to do housing right?

Let's contrast two opposing approaches: authoritarian yet enlightened government policy, and an accidentally anarchic free-for-all.

SINGAPORE: CLEAN LIVING

There's an exception among the festering rot of central planning worldwide: the city-state of Singapore. (Where the author lived for several years.)

Singapore is a heavily regulated society, with low political freedoms. But there's little official corruption—and a great deal of *economic* freedom. In addition to being the sort of place people like to live. Great food, tropical climate, job opportunities, international connections, great food. (It's worth saying twice.)

While there's not much *variety* of housing—most people live in humungous, homogenous tower blocks—it's high-quality. Convenience and communications (like the excellent MRT subway) make everyday life pleasant, and most people are happy with their lot.

But there's a specific reason the tyranny of planning functions there, and it's nothing to do with livable room sizes or modern plumbing. Singapore founder Lee Kuan Yew realised that if you give people a stake in their home—you make it "theirs"—they tend to look after it.

There are complications and exceptions in Singapore's housing policy, but the essence is: ==you don't rent your social housing, you buy it==.

HDB apartments can be mortgaged. There is a market. And market appreciation. On a small island like Singapore, the link between the country's economic success and the value accruing in your personally owned assets is clearer than in most places.

Without much value to start with, Lee and his team realised they had to enable value *creation* for the island's originally poor but hardworking settlers. And that's why it worked. So, if you *have* to have government involvement in housing, the strategy is ==find a way to enable value creation==.

(Not create costs. Which tends to be the outcome of most social housing schemes.)

Singapore looks like the exception. There are very few Singapores. For contrast, let's look at systems *without* any government control, so we can take the best bits of both for our solution.

But first, a cautionary tale from the UK.

Right-to-buy: a great opportunity missed

In the 1980s, British PM Margaret Thatcher put in place the greatest social housing policy ever conceived: right-to-buy. Social housing ("Council") tenants could, if they wished, *buy* the home they'd been renting from government for years, at a decent discount.

Unfortunately, the policy contained one fatal flaw: money from the sale went to *central* government, not local.

In one fell swoop, this destroyed—completely and utterly—any incentive a local council had to build *new* council homes. Because such spending would, in effect, be a time-shifted bung to central government.

Like all public policies, it had far-reaching second-order effects: the Law of Unintended Consequences. (Even if they were entirely foreseeable.)

As always, the best solution in such circumstances is *not to enter the game*. To not *make* such gameable policies in the first place. Which is why government involvement in housing is, excepting one-in-a-thousand places like Singapore, a Bad Thing.

Now: the places where it's happened.

JOY IN THE SLUMS

The old Tung Ling fort in Song Dynasty China had an unusual post-Mao history. For decades, in legal limbo between the PRC and then-British Hong Kong, it housed tens of thousands of people as the Walled City of Kowloon, subject to no official laws or taxes. (Although there were plenty of unofficial ones.)

Families, businesses, and a bare-bones self-governance system that provided some health and social care carried on a hard but viable existence among the Walled City's hundreds of shoulder-width alleyways and ultra-dense 14-storey buildings. Its economy thrived: a third of all dumplings eaten in Hong Kong were produced in its holes-in-the-wall factories.

The Walled City met its end in 1994, but countless examples illustrate what happens in a genuinely unregulated housing market. Brazil's favelas, the suburbs of Nairobi, the slums of Kolkata: all are places which grew simply because people without money were able to build a life there. Over time, many have evolved retail infrastructure, communications, water and garbage systems, healthcare options. All are incredible places full of life and colour.

This isn't to romanticise them. Crime and poverty are rife, and life for most residents is hard. But they illustrate how riotously creative habitable spaces can be, when people have the chance.

There is more joy for the senses in a narrow alley of

==Kolkata than in a hundred square kilometres of American sprawl.==

So how can we get the life-celebrating and freedom-creating aspect of the Brazilian favela as a general principle elsewhere—the creativity unleashed by unregulated growth, yet with the safety and infrastructure of a modern city?

We don't have to look far, because such a place already exists. But let's put that aside for a moment, on the way to a workable solution.

A SOLUTION FOR HOUSING

So: quite a build-up. (Pun intended.) We've seen why the usual go-to for solving problems—"more regulation"—doesn't work outside *very* special cases. However enlightened and well-meant regulations are, increasing complexity by making more of them will create yet more complexity—and worse, *gameability*.

(Gamed systems turn motivations away from the practical objective of providing people with homes. *Always*.)

There are five parts to our solution. Four are subtractive: stripping away distractions and bottlenecks that shouldn't be there. And the last is additive: expanding the scope of what a "home" is.

Just for fun, we'll end with a look at some of those different lifestyles, and how less-explored housing options can be a source not just of a place to sleep, but of joy and pride in a life lived well.

But before those five, a checklist of what a home reasonably needs to include. It's less than you think.

HOUSING AS A SERVICE

The world's biggest retailer, hotel operator, and taxi firm own no products, buildings, or cars. While a house remains a hard product, thinking of your home as a *set of services* is a useful way to decide what matters to *you* when it comes to getting a roof over your head.

The most basic function of a house—walls and a roof—is also the simplest. Research and development of building materials has been going on for 8,000 years, and it's produced some pretty incredible solutions. There are walls that heat themselves. Concrete that flexes in earthquakes. Thin steel structures that can support thousands of tons. Windows that store sunshine. Roofing that harvests rainwater. And that's just some *modern* choices.

From sun-proof adobe to steel-strong bamboo, it's safe to say the safe construction options for any given building span over a thousand choices, if red tape wasn't choking off 99% of them. Making construction methodology a simple best-of-breed decision.

The real value of a home is the *set of services* it offers you. And there's only a few of them. Here's a list.

Electricity. Most basic of all in the modern world, electricity is the difference between a place of shelter and a place to live. It can heat you. Cook your food. Boil your water. It can even *produce* your water: Atmospheric Water Generators capable of sucking 5000L a day out of fresh air are on the market, their water so pure it has to have impurities *added*.

And electricity does this all with a switch, without needing you to chop things, burn things, or get things started inside your home. It's worth a moment's thought about how wonderful and strange this modern superpower really is. With the access it grants to a longer workday, a more comfortable night, and labour-saving appliances, electricity is the basis of a home.

Communications. Electricity's at the top, but this set of services—phone, media, broadband, but also roads and transport—takes second place in the modern home. Even above plumbing.

Because like electricity, the ability to talk (and listen) to the world opens up opportunities to participate in it to your full potential: to find a job, study to improve, even work fulltime from your home.

Comms comes second for this reason: by increasing your radius of choices, it's how you *afford* the home of your dreams.

Plumbing. At last: the water stuff. Hygiene is more than cleanliness: it's health, from drinking 6-8 glasses a day to keeping your work surfaces parasite-free.

That said, water isn't used well in OECD countries. There's nothing more ridiculous than using fresh drinking water to flush toilets, for example: of the average 150L daily water use of a Western adult barely 2% goes into the mouth. Designed accordingly, the water needs of a family home are a lot smaller than you think.

Sewage and garbage. Whether it's burnt, crushed, composted, or collected, a way to remove waste factors high in any home. And again, the right lifestyle means this can be lower on our list than electricity and communications. Even "blackwater" from your toilet doesn't presume heavy public infrastructure: millions of people turn faeces into food by composting their "humanure", while incinerating toilets reduce a family's monthly output to two cups of clean ash. And garbage appliances now in development can do the same for all waste that isn't metal or glass, reducing binfuls of waste to a whisper of dust on the same principle as a self-cleaning oven.

So construction, with modern materials, can be incredibly simple and reliable. And just four basic services, in the mix you prefer, go into the house to make it a worthwhile home.

Yet innovation is stifled by regulation. Hence the first essential part of our solution for housing: turn building *codes* into building *guides*.

FROM CODE TO GUIDE

This book is harsh about planning and regulation and the Nevilles who enforce it. But surprisingly, many such laws are in principle quite *good*.

This is because home is where most people spend most of their lives. Which means paint that expels dangerous fumes over time, or wood that dries to tinder in a decade, are bad ideas for buildings, even if all looks fine on the day of completion. Many laws exist to protect people from such risks.

Yet there's no reason for *government* to be the sole source of laws. So why not rejig the Building Regs … and turn them into building *guidelines*?

Guidelines and best practices exist in many

industries, far from the dead hand of government. Consultancy, software development, the arts: all are largely exempt from regulation, while others—such as most cottage businesses—fly under its radar. That's the *right* way for a market to operate. Because the seller must attract the buyer on the basis of his own reputation and record, not some gamed set of rules and regs.

What does a building guideline look like? They're standards but not solutions. A guideline is "circulation equivalent to 4 changes of air per hour", not "must use extractor fan from Approved Supplier List". Guidelines don't proscribe *how* you do it; they're concerned with the outcome, not the gizmo.

Turning Building Regulations into Building

Guidelines would unleash creativity and innovation in the market, without losing the good bits of those codes that keep people alive and well.

With such a system, you can build whatever you want, to any standard. But if it's against guidelines—or at least fails to meet the parts you consider worthwhile—then your building won't be saleable. And your business won't succeed.

Doing housing right means turning it into a genuine market, where buyers and sellers decide value with the price mechanism matching demand and supply. That's what our solution aims to enable.

So now: the five-part solution itself. With a two-part addendum as a stopgap on the way to solving it fully.

1. Remove planning restrictions

How about this as the basic principle for doing housing right: ==if you own the land, you can build on it==. No zoning, no restrictions, no hassle.

Won't this lead to tower blocks on rural village greens?

No. Because there'll be no demand for them.

With every square metre of private land a potential building plot, the market distortions that lead to identikit suburbs and turn ancient neighbourhoods into human filing cabinets go away. Today in the UK, the difference in price between a one-acre field without building rights and a 1 acre field with planning permission isn't just 10x; it's 50x, 100x,

1,000x. That's the market distortion at the heart of the housing problem: government deciding what you can build, where.

With land a far lower part of overall cost, the incentive for builders—and their market differentiator—is to build a great building, *not* the artificially appreciating land it sits on.

Build a tower block in your back garden if you like. But there'll be no business case for it. Which means your bank won't lend you the money. Nobody will buy the flats it contains, because they'll have a million other choices. Build the wrong building in the wrong place, and you'll lose money. Which no sane person will do.

That's why the first step of our solution—of *any*

solution—must be to ==let the market work==. Because by matching buyers and sellers without distortion, there'll be a far greater number of homes, and a far more interesting variety of them. A building boom—but with all the buildings in the right place, serving market needs.

Enter part 2 of our solution: getting government out of the market.

2. Remove government bungs

All over the world, the opportunity for a developer to build a building relies on bribing local officials.

They call it "providing affordable housing", or "improving local infrastructure", but it's a bung all the same.

This doesn't increase housing supply. As any local housing officer will quietly confirm, it slows them being built in the first place. The more "affordable" units a developer has to build at a loss, the higher the price she has to sell the other units at to cover her costs. And if that price is higher than the market can bear, the building will never be built.

"Socially necessary" is the biggest market distortion

of all. Accordingly, let's get rid of it, as part of the bonfire of regulations this solution proposes. No government giveaways. If the Nevilles want their bungs, they'll have to ask for them the old-fashioned way, in brown envelopes under the table. At least that'll show their true colours.

And by doing so those "affordable" units will be cheaper anyway.

3. Remove taxes ...

Stamp Duty. Sales Taxes. Property levies. They're impediments to moving, logjams between buyer and seller. And they are often *huge*.

In the UK, Stamp Duty adds £12,500 to a London-normal £500,000 house. If it's a second home bought as an investment, that *doubles*. A huge drag on the market.

Economies grow as a function of transactions between people in a market. Taxes reduce the number of those transactions, in addition to being massively unfair. As the third part of our solutions, let's kill off what government charges you for the privilege of buying a house from someone.

3a. ... including taxes on landlords

Socialists often talk starry-eyed of a concept called Rent Control: limiting what landlords can charge tenants by law. They seem to believe this will make housing more affordable.

Economists don't agree on much, but one concept that unites them is: rent control sucks.

All markets have elasticity: the sproinginess of demand and supply. You might think housing is less elastic than most products and services, since the supply (number of houses) is largely fixed, not growing much year on year. That's wrong.

Housing is *extremely* elastic, and not just due to demand. If prices are artificially low, demand goes up, with ten families chasing the same cheap house. Yet the rent the landlord can demand (i.e. the profit he can make) is low by law, meaning the incentive to increase supply (offer more houses to meet demand) is low, too.

So in times of rent control, landlords behave rationally: they set very, very high rents at the start of each tenancy, and strive to make those tenancies as short as possible. It's a basic human trait: you make my life difficult, I'll make yours harder too.

Rent control is the most obscene concept imaginable: two people prevented from entering into a freely agreed contract by Big Government do-gooding. And it doesn't have to be explicit policy. All sorts of taxes and disincentives today make the rental market harder for tenants, by dissuading property owners from offering homes for rent.

Let's do away with all taxes on landlords that aren't levied on normal income. In all their forms. And in doing so, increase supply and consumer choice, the way a free market always does.

4. Lose adverse aversions

Part 3 of our solution showed us the number of houses isn't a fixed supply. The surprise: the supply of land itself isn't fixed, either.

Some 15% of the UK's land area is not owned by anyone. (Often because someone died heirless.) Amazingly, under adverse possession laws, anyone can legally fence such land off, stake a claim, and demonstrate they've put it into use as part of a process to gain ownership. It takes many years, but it's possible. While across the Atlantic, vast areas of the USA and Canada are for sale for pennies.

It's cheap (or free) because it's "useless land". The point here: the definition of "useless" is "legally barred from using it", not "without value".

Most of these scraps of land—rural, inaccessible, far from roads—would have plenty of potential to someone interested in growing their own food and living off-grid. If only there weren't so many building regulations and so on. Which is our solution there aren't.

That's our fourth idea: turn adverse possession from an abstruse legal point to a normal and acceptable way to acquire your own land and put it into use.

After all, nobody else is staking a claim to it. Would you *really* rather government owned it?

5. Think Tiny

We typically use barely 20% of our floorspace. Millions of Americans forgo McMansion ambitions for life on a trailer. Walk around any IKEA and you'll see livable apartments as small as 250 sq ft.

Countless people—including landless young singles in cities—would be perfectly happy with far less space if it meant they could own their own home earlier in life and at lower cost.

This is the idea behind the **Tiny House Movement**: the deliberate decision to live big in less space. (Search YouTube for countless examples and inspirations.)

The general agreement is that a Tiny House is under 400 square feet. You can fit a lot more of those onto a building plot than current government regulations would permit. And 400sqft is larger than many think.

With sleeping lofts or a second floor, it allows more than one bedroom and bathroom, a full kitchen and living area, plenty of storage. Modern technology—flatscreen TVs, LED lighting—takes up less space anyway. And such buildings take less energy to power. Consume fewer resources. Many can even be moved, leaving even less impact on Mother Earth.

So our fifth and last idea is a change in mindset: enable smaller spaces as homes, and embed the idea that more footage means more value. Let's recall that a "high" population density—like Singapore's 8,000 per square kilometre—doesn't feel cramped.

(… and the stopgap solution)

Of course, the removal of all planning restrictions would unleash a frenzy of market-driven housing solutions. Most of them good—but not all. So our Big Solution in five parts isn't going to fly with any government imaginable today. Much less any Neville anxious to hold onto his power.

But there's a stopgap solution that might just work. It's even in play in some countries today.

Here it is: you get all the bits of our five-leg solution—no planning restrictions, no building codes, no zoning laws, and no Nevilles—as long as you build on your own land … and whatever you build *leaves no trace.*

Build big, build small. Build short, build tall. Build back-to-nature or build high-tech. But whatever you build, it must be removeable from the land without leaving a mark, and must not be connected to any external infrastructure.

Which means most—if not all—such buildings would be lightweight, economical, off-grid, and on wheels. No concrete foundations, no service infrastructure, no rolling your own roads. Buildings that sit lightly on the land, yet provide real homes at low cost. And within those limits, scope for amazing creativity.

Now *that's* a market opportunity. As millions of Tiny Homers and off-grid homesteaders have shown.

(and make better use of architects)

The other half of our stopgap solution is more outcome than policy: a building boom means a greater need for architects. People whose profession combines engineering with art. *Precisely* the right folk to address housing issues with *creativity*.

So: if you're worried about monstrous carbuncles arising in heritage areas, let's add a second point to our leave-no-trace stopgapper: *all buildings must be designed by a qualified architect*.

Wouldn't it be great if—instead of poring over regulations and codes—these artists-in-turtlenecks could make even the meanest home a work of art?

ADDENDUM

That's how to do housing. Get rid of Big Government meddling and let the market work. Same as any other solution, really: remove the coercive nature of the power relationship government enables, and let people transact in accordance with their natures, trading value for value.

Of course, the journey will be a long one. And with authoritarianism rising around the world, it'll probably get worse before it gets better. But some people *are* beating the system—and thriving in a variety of unconventional living situations. Before we finally get to that closest ideal of riotous creativity in the world today, let's touch on a few.

Going Tiny

Tiny Homes often follow a standard layout: watery stuff at one end (kitchen and bathroom), a long lounge, and bedroom lofts above, plus a nice deck outside for outdoor living. Many are THOWs (Tiny Houses on Wheels) and can be moved around: a typical size is 28ft in length, with some going over 45.

It's a sensible financial option. In the USA, 68% of Tiny owners own their homes outright. 55% have more savings than the average American.

There is a caveat. Many young owners park on their parent's land. Or are sucking their electricity. Taking advantage of perks the type of people who *really* need low-cost housing don't have.

But the homes themselves are often creative, beautiful, and life-affirming. Just what a house needs to feel like a home.

Containing yourself

Thanks to international trade, there are approximately 100 million starter homes in kit form lying around at ports. They're called "shipping containers".

A shipping container is strong—almost unbelievably so—yet light, making use of corrugations that let a standard twenty-foot equivalent unit (TEU) carry 25,000kg with walls just 1.6mm thick. They're already weatherproof, because they're designed to sit on the deck of a ship at sea. They're kitted out for being put on a trailer and moved around, because this is how intermodal freight operates. While being made of Corten steel makes them customisable to a T, with windows and doors to suit.

Most importantly, at 150sq ft, a standard TEU is about the size of a liveable room. A clever 20ft layout makes a home for one; a 40ft container can house a family if well designed.

Combine these with solar panels, just add water, and you've got modular housing for the Information Age.

Vanlife

Some 100,000 people in the USA are living full-time by choice in the tinest homes of all. Once, it might have been called homelessness. Today, it's a chic cliché of sun-bronzed twentysomethings doing Yoga on a beach at dawn.

#vanlife started in the USA, although it's been around at least since the 60s (and arguably goes back to travelling communities from India to Ireland.) What it demonstrates is that it *is* possible to live a quality life—with electricity, communications, plumbing, and waste management—in a vehicle with accommodation the size of two double beds.

Again, there are caveats. Search YouTube for the

latest on van living, and you'll notice is that they're all white: the people at the forefront of the movement tend to be middle-class or above and doing it by choice. (Most people living in their vehicles aren't.) But the vehicles themselves are fascinating explorations of creativity, merging two basic human drivers: the need to feel at home, and the need to see the world.

Tiny Houses, container homes, even Vanlife demonstrate there's a broader choice of housing options—if regulations would just permit them.

As our final thought, let's look (finally) at that place where it all sort-of comes together today. It's perhaps not where you thought.

TICKET TO TOKYO

Japan is a crowded country without much buildable land. For a brief moment in the boomtown 80s, the land area of Tokyo was worth more than the entire USA. As Japan's largest city, it still attracts all sorts: young from the nation's emptying rural areas, foreigners at both ends of the wage scale, millions of salarymen commuting for hours each day. Streets are narrow, services are strung across streets in wire bundles, and average home sizes are small.

Yet Tokyo doesn't have a housing problem.

In this most expensive of cities, a student can still find a private apartment for under $500/mth. That tiny space will nonetheless have easy access to shops, stations, services that add value to life. And it's all because of Tokyo's policies at our macro, meso, and micro levels.

Or—rather—the lack of policies.

There isn't much zoning in japanese cities. And few controls on what you can build on land you own. So services arise where they're needed. For such a bureaucratic society, restrictions are few. That's why Tokyo serves as a partial model of what our solution for housing might enable.

A street in Tokyo will contain houses. Apartment blocks. A 7-11. Multiple shops and noodle bars. A row of vending machines. A police box. Places to work. Places to relax. Places to meet friends.

What's more the architectural styles are

extraordinarily varied. You'll see concrete zombie-bunkers. Old wooden shophouses. Glass baubles. Traditional teahouses. Tiled curiosities made from puzzle parts. Offices. Family businesses. Kiosks.

And this would be a single street.

From the central circle enclosed by the Yamanote line to the outer wards where people live, Tokyo is an endless visual feast.

There is one restriction: if you inherit a house, the law subjects it to heavy taxes after 30 years. The burden is so heavy, in fact, that it's normal to knock down your parents' house and build a new one of your own. Which means building materials are often short-term: lightweight, flimsy, designed for a span measured in decades not generations. But they're perfect for the time people want to live in them, which is now.

Le Corbusier only visited Japan once, long after his famous quote "A house is a machine for living in." But Tokyo demonstrates his principle well. Far from perfect everywhere, lots of ineffiencies and mismatches, but gloriously functional—and alive.

Without the cold dead hand of over-regulation, and the desires of customers taking precedence over the preferences of government, everyone who wants to live well can do so—and do so at reasonable cost.

Let's make it happen.

ABOUT CHRIS

Chris Worth is a London-based copywriter and author of the guide to effective freelancing **100 Days, 100 Grand**. Google it or head for 100days100grand.com.

At work, he creates campaigns and content backed by meaningful insights, mostly for technology clients. (He does the research and analysis too, btw—his USP.)

Interests include adventure travel and extreme sports. He's lived in six countries, visited 60, and is a qualified sky and scuba diver with a passion for calisthenics and kettlebells. But he's never without his Kindle. See him at chrisdoescontent.com.

www.ingramcontent.com/pod-product-compliance
Lightning Source LLC
Chambersburg PA
CBHW081354080526
44588CB00016B/2499